W9-CKI-087

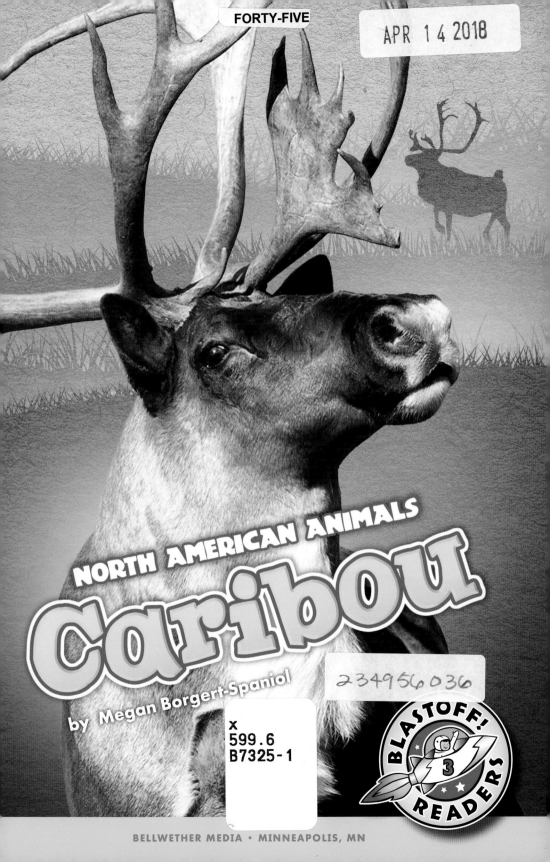

NORTH AMERICAN ANIMALS

Caribou

by Megan Borgert-Spaniol

BLASTOFF! READERS
3

BELLWETHER MEDIA • MINNEAPOLIS, MN

Note to Librarians, Teachers, and Parents:

Blastoff! Readers are carefully developed by literacy experts and combine standards-based content with developmentally appropriate text.

Level 1 provides the most support through repetition of high-frequency words, light text, predictable sentence patterns, and strong visual support.

Level 2 offers early readers a bit more challenge through varied simple sentences, increased text load, and less repetition of high-frequency words.

Level 3 advances early-fluent readers toward fluency through increased text and concept load, less reliance on visuals, longer sentences, and more literary language.

Level 4 builds reading stamina by providing more text per page, increased use of punctuation, greater variation in sentence patterns, and increasingly challenging vocabulary.

Level 5 encourages children to move from "learning to read" to "reading to learn" by providing even more text, varied writing styles, and less familiar topics.

Whichever book is right for your reader, Blastoff! Readers are the perfect books to build confidence and encourage a love of reading that will last a lifetime!

This edition first published in 2018 by Bellwether Media, Inc.

No part of this publication may be reproduced in whole or in part without written permission of the publisher. For information regarding permission, write to Bellwether Media, Inc., Attention: Permissions Department, 5357 Penn Avenue South, Minneapolis, MN 55419.

Library of Congress Cataloging-in-Publication Data

LC record for Caribou available at https://lccn.loc.gov/2016052748

Editor: Nathan Sommer   Designer: Josh Brink

Printed in the United States of America, North Mankato, MN.

Table of Contents

Caribou are a large type of deer. They roam forests, mountains, and **tundra** in Greenland, Canada, Alaska, and northern Washington.

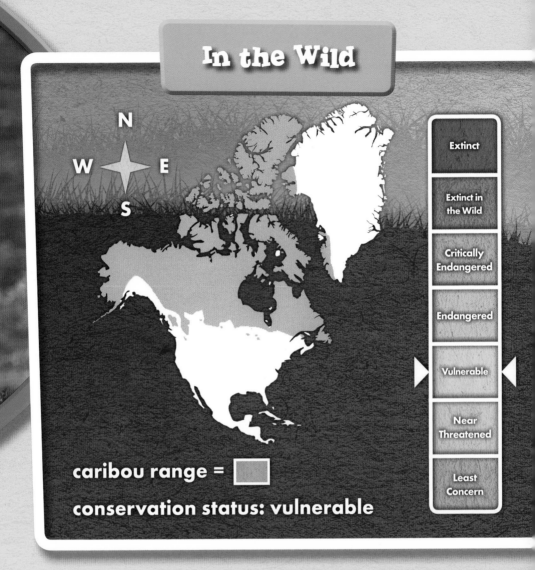

In the Wild

N
W E
S

caribou range = ▢

conservation status: vulnerable

Extinct

Extinct in the Wild

Critically Endangered

Endangered

Vulnerable

Near Threatened

Least Concern

Outside of North America, these **mammals** are called reindeer.

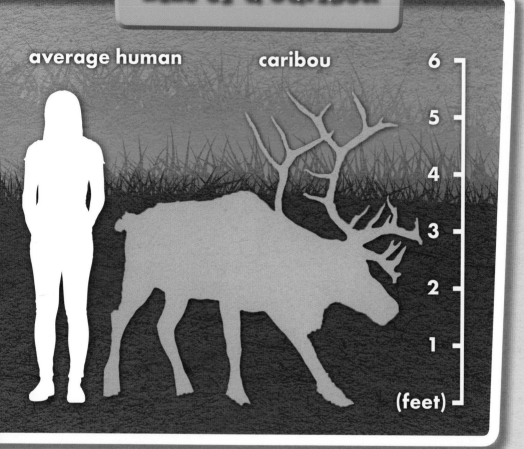

average human   caribou

6
5
4
3
2
1
(feet)

Caribou stand about 4 feet (1.2 meters) tall. Males can weigh up to 700 pounds (318 kilograms).

They are sometimes double the size of females!

Thick double coats protect caribou against the wind and cold of their **habitats**. Long, **hollow** hairs cover soft undercoats.

split hooves   **thick double coat**   **long antlers**

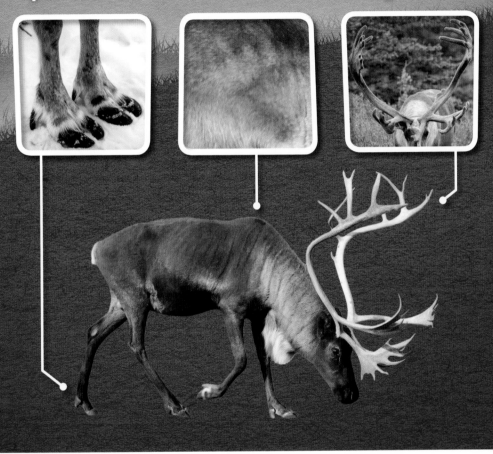

Split hooves help caribou move over snow and ice.

9

antlers

All male and some female caribou have **antlers**. The antlers fall off each year and grow back larger in winter or spring.

A male's antlers can be more
than 4 feet (1.2 meters) long!

herd

Twice a year, caribou **migrate** hundreds of miles. **Herds** move north for the summer to feed on tundra plants.

In winter, they escape the cold wind and deep snow of the tundra. Herds travel south to find food and shelter.

Caribou are **herbivores**. They eat grass, moss, and other tundra plants during summer.

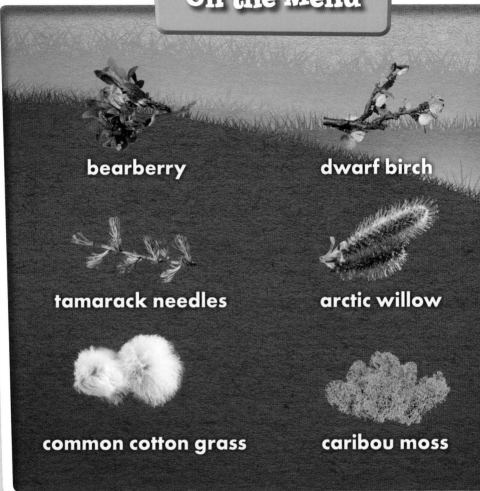

bearberry

dwarf birch

tamarack needles

arctic willow

common cotton grass

caribou moss

In winter, caribou dig **lichens** from the snow with their hooves and antlers. They can eat up to 12 pounds (5.4 kilograms) of food a day!

Caribou often feed in large herds. This helps keep **predators** away.

gray wolves

grizzly bears

wolverines

golden eagles

They must watch out for hungry grizzly bears and gray wolves.

Caribou Calves

Female caribou give birth to **calves** each spring. The calves grow fast! They run with mom after a few hours and can **graze** at one week old.

Baby Facts

Name for babies:	calves
Size of litter:	1 or 2 calves
Length of pregnancy:	7 to 8 months
Time spent with mom:	about 6 months

Soon, their antlers begin
to grow.

The antlers start as small bumps.
They will grow bigger every year!

Glossary

antlers—branched bones on the heads of some animals; antlers look like horns.

calves—baby caribou

graze—to feed on plants on the ground

habitats—lands with certain types of plants, animals, and weather

herbivores—animals that eat only plants

herds—groups of caribou that travel together; there can be hundreds of caribou in a herd.

hollow—empty through the middle; a caribou's hollow hairs trap air to keep it warm.

lichens—plantlike living things that grow on rocks and trees

mammals—warm-blooded animals that have backbones and feed their young milk

migrate—to travel from one place to another, often with the seasons

predators—animals that hunt other animals for food

split hooves—hooves that are split into two toes; hooves are hard coverings that protect the feet of some animals.

tundra—dry land where the ground is frozen year-round

To Learn More

AT THE LIBRARY
Hirsch, Rebecca E., and Maria Koran. *Caribou: A Tundra Journey.* New York, N.Y.: AV2 by Weigl, 2017.

Jeffries, Joyce. *Caribou.* New York, N.Y.: PowerKids Press, 2016.

Marsico, Katie. *Reindeer.* Chicago, Ill.: Heinemann Library, 2012.

ON THE WEB
Learning more about caribou is as easy as 1, 2, 3.

1. Go to www.factsurfer.com.

2. Enter "caribou" into the search box.

3. Click the "Surf" button and you will see a list of related web sites.

With factsurfer.com, finding more information is just a click away.

Index

The images in this book are reproduced through the courtesy of: Donald M. Jones/ SuperStock, front cover; Ron Niebrugge/ Alamy, p. 4; Howard Sandler, p. 7; Mircea C, pp. 8, 9 (top center), 14; STEPANOV ILYA, p. 9 (top left); Menno Schaefer, p. 9 (top right); Iakov Filimonov, p. 9 (bottom); Pim Leijen, p. 10; Jeff McGraw, p. 11; Alaska Stock/ age fotostock, p. 12; Colin Monteath/ age fotostock, p. 13; HHelene, p. 15 (top left, top right); Janne Skinnarla, p. 15 (center left); Alexander Piragis, p. 15 (center right); Nicram Sabod, p. 15 (bottom left); Madlen, p. 15 (bottom right); Sergey Krasnoshchokov, p. 16; Max K, p. 17 (top left); Nagel Photography, p. 17 (top right); Stayer, p. 17 (bottom left); withGod, p. 17 (bottom right); Wayne Lynch/ age fotostock, pp. 18, 20; Alexey Seafarer, p. 19; Arildina, p. 21.